Fast, Faster, Fastest

by Michael Dahl
illustrated by Brian Jensen

Animals Th... ...Speeds

PICTURE WINDOW BOOKS
Minneapolis, Minnesota

Editorial Director: Carol Jones
Managing Editor: Catherine Neitge
Creative Director: Keith Griffin
Editor: Christianne Jones
Story Consultant: Terry Flaherty
Designer: Nathan Gassman
Production Artist: Angela Kilmer
Page Production: Picture Window Books
The illustrations in this book were created with pastels.

Picture Window Books
5115 Excelsior Boulevard, Suite 232
Minneapolis, MN 55416
877-845-8392
www.picturewindowbooks.com

Printed in the United States of America.

Library of Congress Cataloging-in-Publication Data
Dahl, Michael.
Fast, faster, fastest : animals that move at great speeds /
written by Michael Dahl ; illustrated by Brian Jensen.
p. cm. — (Animal extremes)
Includes bibliographical references and index.
ISBN 1-4048-1172-9 (hardcover)
1. Animal locomotion—Juvenile literature. I. Jensen, Brian.
II. Title.

QP301.D243 2006
573.7'9—dc22   2005003733

Thanks to our advisers for their expertise, research, and advice:

Dr. James F. Hare, Associate Professor of Zoology
University of Manitoba
Winnipeg, Manitoba

Susan Kesselring, M.A., Literacy Educator
Rosemount-Apple Valley-Eagan (Minnesota) School District

Animals move everywhere. They fly over the highest mountains and dive through the deepest oceans. They run over the hottest deserts and swim in the coldest waters.

Don't blink, or you might miss these animals that can move at extreme speeds. Watch the needle move across the speedometer as you turn each page.

Hop! Hop! Hop!

The kangaroo bounces 35 mph across the dusty deserts of Australia.

Can any animal move faster?

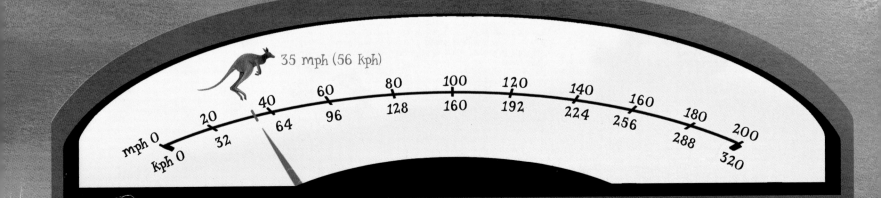

35 mph (56 Kph)

mph 0   20   40   60   80   100   120   140   160   180   200

Kph 0   32   64   96   128   160   192   224   256   288   320

Yes! The zebra can! Its black and white stripes zoom across the African plains at 40 mph.

Can any animal move faster?

40 mph (64 Kph)

mph	0	20	40	60	80	100	120	140	160	180	200
Kph	0	32	64	96	128	160	192	224	256	288	320

Yes! The lion can! It sprints 50 mph along the savanna in southern Africa.

Can any animal move faster?

50 mph (80 kph)

mph 0   20   40   60   80   100   120   140   160   180   200

kph 0   32   64   96   128   160   192   224   256   288   320

Yes! The pronghorn can!

10

It whisks 60 mph across the plains of North America.

Can any animal move faster?

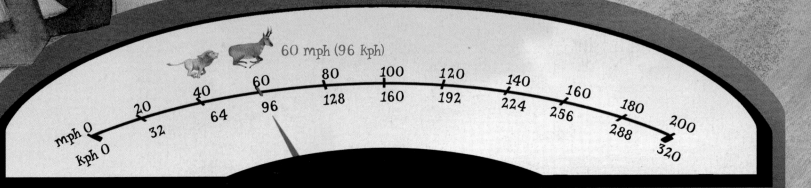

60 mph (96 kph)

mph 0   20   40   60   80   100   120   140   160   180   200
Kph 0   32   64   96   128   160   192   224   256   288   320

Yes! A cheetah can! It races after its supper at 70 mph across eastern Africa.

Can any animal move faster?

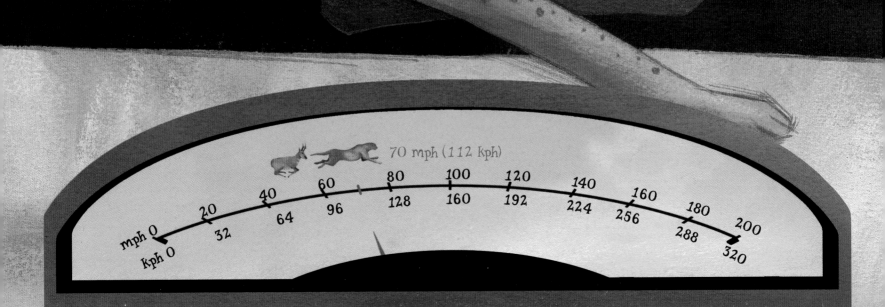

70 mph (112 kph)

mph 0   20   40   60   80   100   120   140   160   180   200
Kph 0   32   64   96   128   160   192   224   256   288   320

Yes! A white-throated needle-tailed swift can! It dives 106 mph over a waterfall in central Asia.

14

Can any animal move faster?

106 mph (170 kph)

mph 0   20   40   60   80   100   120   140   160   180   200
kph 0   32   64   96   128   160   192   224   256   288   320

16

Yes! A bald eagle can! It swoops down at 185 mph over the tall trees of North America.

Can any animal move faster?

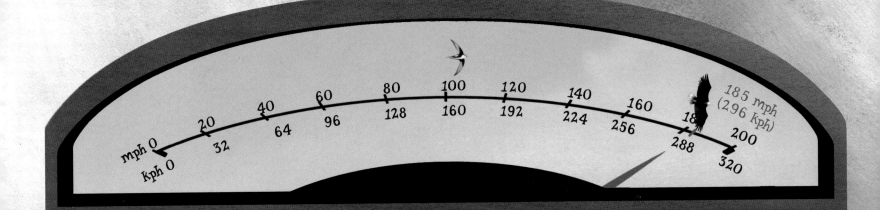

mph 0   20   40   60   80   100   120   140   160   18   185 mph
                                                                   (296 Kph)
Kph 0   32   64   96   128   160   192   224   256   288   200   320

18

Yes! A peregrine falcon can! It flies 217 mph over the Canadian forests.

Can any animal move faster?

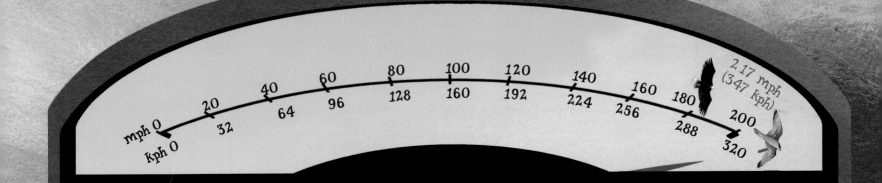

mph 0   20   40   60   80   100   120   140   160   180   217 mph (347 Kph)   200

Kph 0   32   64   96   128   160   192   224   256   288   320

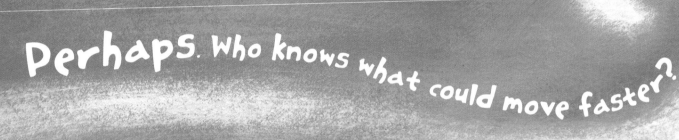

Perhaps. Who knows what could move faster?

20

Extreme Fun Facts

kangaroo

Most kangaroos can not move one leg at a time. They have to move them together. To help them when they move slowly, they use their tails as an extra leg.

zebra

Each zebra has a unique pattern of stripes. The stripes can be narrow or wide.

lion

Lions nap, sleep, or rest for 21 hours a day! They have small bursts of energy they use for hunting, but they are usually laying around.

pronghorn

The pronghorn is the only horned animal in the world that sheds at least the outer layer of its horns every year.

cheetah

When cheetahs run, it looks like they are flying! Between strides, all four legs are in the air.

white-throated needle-tailed swift

The white-throated needle-tailed swift spends most of its life in the air. It never lands on the ground on purpose.

bald eagle

Bald eagles aren't bald. Their heads are covered with short white feathers. Their name came from the English word "balde," which means white.

peregrine falcon

Peregrine falcons nest on every continent except Antarctica. They leave their nests in the winter, but return to the same nest each summer.

Glossary

plains—*flat land with few trees*

savanna—*flat, grassy plain with few trees*

soar—*to fly high in the air*

sprint—*to run fast for a short distance*

swoop—*to dive down suddenly*

whisk—*to move quickly*

zoom—*to move suddenly and quickly*

To Learn More

At the Library

Behm, Barbara. *Quick and Slow Animals.* Milwaukee: Gareth Stevens Pub., 1999.

Bullard, Lisa. *Fast and Slow: An Animal Opposites Book.* Mankato, Minn.: Capstone Press, 2006.

Harris, Nicholas. *How Fast?* Farmington Hills, Mich.: Blackbirch Press, 2004.

On the Web

FactHound offers a safe, fun way to find Web sites related to this book. All of the sites on FactHound have been researched by our staff.
www.facthound.com

1. Visit the FactHound home page.

2. Enter a search word related to this book, or type in this special code: 1404811729

3. Click on the FETCH IT button.

Your trusty FactHound will fetch the best sites for you!

Index

Look for all of the books in the Animal Extremes series:

Cold, Colder, Coldest: *Animals That Adapt to Cold Weather*

Deep, Deeper, Deepest: *Animals That Go to Great Depths*

Fast, Faster, Fastest: *Animals That Move at Great Speeds*

High, Higher, Highest: *Animals That Go to Great Heights*

Hot, Hotter, Hottest: *Animals That Adapt to Great Heat*

Old, Older, Oldest: *Animals That Live Long Lives*